The Brancacci Chapel

The Brancacci Chapel

Electa

How to use this guide.

Introduction
The first part of the guide
gives a brief historical outline
of the building and growth
of the Brancacci Chapel.

The Visit
The second part of the guide
lists the artists and describes
the single scenes frescoed
in the Chapel. A complete
technical description is given
for each scene.

Appendices
The last part of the guide
includes an interesting essay
on the restoration of the
Brancacci Chapel. Then there
is a biography of the artists
of the frescoes, followed by
a selected bibliography.

On the Cover
Masaccio and Filippino Lippi,
*The Raising of the Son
of Theophilus and Saint Peter
Enthroned* (detail).

The texts were taken from
the volume *Cappella Brancacci*
by Umberto Baldini and Ornella
Casazza,Olivetti-Electa, Milan 1990,
and revised for this guide
by Franco Ambrosio.

Translation
Richard Sadleir

Photographs
Antonio Quattrone, Florence

©1991, by **Electa**, Milan
Elemond Editori Associati
All rights reserved
Revised edition 1996

Contents

The Brancacci Chapel from Its Foundation to the Present

The chapel stands at the end of the right arm of the transept of the church of Santa Maria del Carmine in Florence. It has a rectangular ground plan and is 6.84 metres deep (including the entrance pillar) and 5.68 wide. It is dedicated to the*"Madonna del Carmine"* (Our Lady of Mount Carmel) or the *"Madonna del Popolo."*

It was under the patronage of the Brancacci family, which kept it from the mid-14th century up until 1780, when it passed down to the Riccardi.

Its history begins with Piero di Piuvichese Brancacci, whose testament, dated 20 February 1367, desired "the foundation of a family chapel as a certain and acknowledged testimony to the standing of the family and a symbol of its solid prosperity" (Pandemiglio 1987). But it was his son Antonio who actually made a start on construction. Reliable evidence of work in progress appears only in March 1387.

Felice de Michele was the patron of the chapel from 1422 until at least 1436. A wealthy, powerful man, Felice Brancacci held important public offices, including that of ambassador to Egypt in 1422. It was on his return from Cairo in February 1423 that he entrusted the decoration of the chapel to Masolino and Masaccio. (Felice was certainly responsible for the choice of the subject of the *Stories of Saint Peter,* linked in many ways with his own notifications of merchandise.)

Here we will have to glance aside for a moment to examine the relationship between Masolino and Masaccio. In 1423 Masolino was forty years old and Masaccio only twenty-two, though he had already produced some outstanding works. For a long time it was taken for granted, given the difference in age, that they were master and pupil whose collaboration soon came to an end when the master became an unequal, absent partner. Misgivings about this "orthodox," version were based on a single clue: the *Festival*, a fresco painted in the Carmine cloisters in 1422 and now lost, but with abundant surviving evidence for its existence in drawn copies. In it, Masaccio is portrayed together with Masolino; the two figures stand out sharply with their intense gaze fixed on the viewer. This shows that at that date they were definitely still associated with each other, and it is highly likely that a natural and complementary sympathy must have bound them together; it is inconceivable that Masaccio would have consented to allow anyone else to share in a work of such decisive importance as this merely for the sake of practical advantages and without any esteem for the other person. And in fact, even after the restoration, the equilibrium in the whole, despite the differences, is remarkable, so that L. Berti has compared it to a "great duet" (Berti 1988).

Returning to the chronology, the present state of the chapel and then *Stories* is the fruit of rearrangements and modifications undertaken initially to enable Masaccio and Masolino to paint the frescoes and then continued in the period when Felice Brancacci fell from grace (1436) as well as later in the 18th and 19th centuries.

Masolino, The Healing of the Lame Man and The Raising of Tabitha *(detail).*

The pictorial wall decorations.   At the start of the restoration work (in 1981) a window was discovered. It had two lights and was markedly elongated in shape: the chapel was originally illuminated by the light it shed. The aperture of the window was reduced in size to provide a new wall surface above the altar large enough for the last scene in the *Stories of Saint Peter.*

The next changes were made between 1435 and 1458. To eliminate any possible sign of anti-Medici sentiment attributable to Felice, the Carmelite friars effaced the likenesses of all the figures representing the Brancacci family, painted by Masaccio in the *Raising of the Son of Theophilus.*

In 1481 and 1482 Filippino Lippi carried out thorough restoration work and completion of the stories and figures still missing.

Other modifications to the chapel were carried out in 1670 and subsequent years with the addition to the division in the first order of a carved wooden cornice and four similar large figures to support it.

The next change came in 1674, with the "addition of a white marble plinth with back rests running all round the chapel, together with the paving and altar steps, also of marble, and the bannisters" (Procacci 1984).

On this occasion, together with the addition of furnishings and general "embellishments," it is likely that the leaves were painted to hide the nakedness of Adam and Eve in the scene representing the *Original Sin* and the *Expulsion*

from Eden, respectively by Masolino and Masaccio. The leaves are not part of the original paintings, as is proved decisively by the material used and the fact that they are painted on the surface of the plaster. Telethermographic examination, using infra-red rays, was used to view the original paintwork below, and the bodies were found to be naked. There is no precise record of when the leaves were added or by whom, but it was certainly not long before the reign of Cosimo III, whose bigotry is well known, and they may actually have been added during his reign.

In 1680 Marchese Francesco Ferroni offered to purchase the chapel and refashion it in the manner of the Corsini Chapel on the other side of the transept, after destroying the frescoes, whose style was now regarded as "outmoded." But the opposition of Grand Duchess Vittoria Della Rovere led to the failure of the project.

There are references to the decayed state of the frescoes in a manuscript record (see Procacci 1984, p. 10) which also reveals that the *Stories* were no longer an object of worship; the document expresses appreciation of them but only as "very old paintings."

In 1734 new architectural decorations were added to the church; at the same time many of the wall paintings were cleaned, as well as the Chapel of the Madonna by the painter Antonio Pillori.

In 1746–1748 there were further thoughtless changes made

to the chapel, due to the intervention of Angiola Tempesti, the mother of the prior Lorenzo Gasparo Masini. Work was first carried out on the outside wall of the chapel, which was decorated with stucco and masonry; the work was completed in 1747 but was regarded such with disfavour that it was removed and replaced by stonework designed by the French architect Chaman.

Work was then done in the interior. The vault, already badly damaged by damp according to Richa, was totally destroyed, and with it the frescoes of the Evangelist painted, so the records relate, by Masolino. The frescoes in the lunettes were also removed because, it was said, "they are of no merit."

The operation was conducted by Vincenzo Meucci, who decorated the vault with *The Madonna Giving the Scapular to Saint Simon Stock*, and by Carlo Sacconi, who decorated the lunettes at the sides with architectural motifs.

Next came the disastrous fire on the night of 28 January 1771. It devasted the church but without causing any serious or irreparable damage to the Brancacci Chapel. A contemporary record says that the blaze "did not cause irreparable damage to that [painting] in the chapel formerly of the Brancacci family known as the Chapel of the Madonna." "Irreparable" here means the total loss of the painting; but the recent studies have shown that irreparable damage was caused by the heat of the fire to various parts of the *Stories*, resulting in extensive and irrecuperable changes to certain colours.

A few days after the fire, on February 3, the architects Giuseppe Salvetti and Romualdo Morozzi, examined the damaged church by order of the superiors. It was then decided to reglaze the window and close off the opening in the façade with timber. The cleaning and retouching were the work of Giuseppe Romei, according to the account given by Abbé Vincenzo Follini, who was an eye-witness of events. Romei was the artist who had painted the great vault of the transept of the church.

On 18 August 1780 Marchese Gabriello Riccardi—a Canonical Dean—paid two thousand *scudi* for the chapel after negotiations with the Granducal commissioner, Giovanni Battista Cangini, commissioned to act as intermediary between the old and new patrons of the various chapels in the church following the fire and the relinquishment of the patronage of the chapel by the Brancacci family.

The restoration work was limited to the vault of the *sepolcreto* below (the only one to have been badly damaged by the fire), which was completely renovated, and the paving and cladding of the lower part of the chapel. The old altar, badly damaged by the flames, was replaced.

When work was completed in 1782, Canon Gabriello had a plaque set in the floor before the altar; it still exists and testifies to one of the last acts of patronage of the Riccardi family, who helped preserve the precious frescoes by Masaccio, well aware that they were saving a valuable piece of the history of Florence threatened by time and the acts of men. It is not until 1830 that we have any information on the fate of the chapel in the 19th century. An eminent scholar, Attilio Zuccagni Orlandini wrote, a report on the condition "of one of the most precious monuments of the many that enhance this city." It concluded with a pressing request that further restoration work should be undertaken as soon as possible. This is the first of a long series of records, surveys, and letters forwarded to the authorities with the aim of securing the restoration of the frescoes in the Brancacci Chapel. All that came of them was the designation of Pietro Pezzati on 16 January 1865 as restorer of the frescoes. But nothing came of this appointment, partly because the committee formed for the purpose resigned since it lacked the powers to be effective and above all because there were no funds available for the work.

But something must have been done in these same years because a letter written at the beginning of this century by the architect in charge of the Regional Office for the Conservation of the Monuments of Tuscany stated that "the celebrated frescoes [have not been] cleaned since they were strengthened about fifty years ago."

In 1890 there is a reference to the fact that "the marble decorations on the walls, whose white mass upset the harmony of the interior and made it difficult to view the splendid frescoes, have been covered with timber and the floor, which is also white, is to be covered with a carpet with muted colours."

On 18 May 1895, an earthquake struck the city of Florence, causing damage to the church and convent; a report sent by the Regional Office for the Conservation of Monuments to the Ministry shows this to have been very limited in extent and immediately repaired.

At the start of this century new and authoritative voices were raised to demand improvements to the state of the paintings by Masaccio, Masolino, Panicale and Filippino Lippi and measures to ensure their safety.

On 30 June 1904 a survey was carried out by a sub-committee appointed by the Commission for the Preservation of Monuments and Excavations of the Prefecture. Following this the Minister gave his approval to "a simple general removal of dust from the frescoes" and permitted the work to be entrusted to the restorer Filippo Fiscali.

In October work began; it was completed by 29 November and on 6 December the inspectors' report was drafted. It "expressed unanimously pleasure and satisfaction for the diligent and conscientious manner in which the frescoes have been cleaned by *signor* Filippo Fiscali."

During World War I, the plan for defending works of art against war damage caused the frescoes to be protected by piles of sandbags and covered with strips of canvas or cardboard. However, the church was used as a military storehouse and a wall was built to separate the chapel from the rest of the church. But then further orders were given to protect the works of art more carefully and "totally isolate the transept from the rest of the church." To this end "the wall was demolished and rebuilt at the edge of the nave of the church."

In 1928 plans were made for further restoration but nothing came of them.

In 1929–1930 the aperture of the window was enlarged, the proportions of the 18th century Baroque altar were reduced and the paving relaid.

Finally, in 1932, during the search for old frescoes in the church, the two small projections of the marble altar were removed, so revealing two small areas of fresco belonging to the *Stories* (the scenes of *Saint Peter Baptizing the Neophytes* and *Saint Peter Preaching*): these served to show the shades of the colours when the altar was built soon after 1748. In the following years very cautious experiments were made with the cleaning of tiny patches of fresco.

In November 1946 the roof over the Brancacci Chapel caved in when a beam broke, allowing water to pour in; but repairs were made immediately, before irreparable damage occurred. No other significant events occurred in subsequent years, but the rapid "darkening" of the frescoes caused by the degeneration of the substances spread over their surfaces and aggravated by air pollution in the 1970s led to the chapel being placed under the control of the Opificio delle Pietre Dure, which began to take readings of humidity and temperature to enable a continuous check to be kept on the variations in the state of the frescoes in the changes of weather and the seasons.

The state of preservation of the chapel is kept under control by instruments capable of providing objective and concrete data. Analyses are made so as to create a "clinical case history," a basis for decisions about when and how to intervene to protect the frescoes.

But first of all it was necessary to collect all the possible information that could be gleaned from the walls of the chapel, quite apart from the restoration work and changes made before and after the 1771 fire.

In 1981 restoration work began and was completed in 1990. This memorable intervention has removed the thick coat of smoke and grime veiling the fresco, returning its colours to their original splendour.

When the Brancacci Chapel was reopened to the public it had been given a separate entrance from the church of Santa Maria del Carmine. To gain access one now passes through a pleasing 17th-century cloister, around which open important rooms of the ancient Carmelite convent containing interesting frescoes from the 14th to the 16th century.

Masaccio and Filippino Lippi,
*The Raising of the Son
of Theophilus and Saint Peter
Enthroned* (detail).

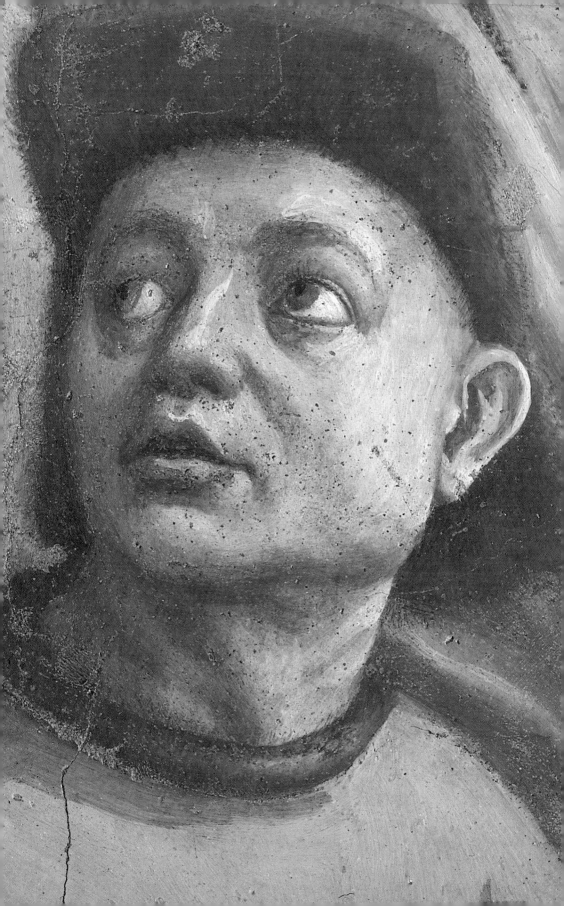

Masolino
*Adam and Eve
in the Earthly Paradise
and The Temptation*

"And the Lord God planted a garden eastward of Eden; and there he put the man whom he had formed. And out of the ground made the Lord God to grow every tree that is pleasant to the sight, and good for food; the tree of life also in the midst of the garden, and the tree of knowledge of good and evil" (Genesis, 2, 8–9).

"And when the woman saw that the tree was good for food, and that it was pleasant to the eyes, and a tree to be desired to make one wise, she took of the fruit thereof, and did eat, and gave also unto her husband with her; and he did eat" (Genesis, 3, 6).

Eve has just plucked a fruit from the tree and is holding it in her right hand. The serpent is twined about the tree, which is a fig tree with the typical deeply lobed leaves. The fruit that Eve has plucked, like those that can be glimpsed among the foliage, retains only slight traces of its original reddish-brown colour.

It is highly likely that the tradition identifying the fig tree with the tree of knowledge is Mediterranean or Oriental and the "apple" is a North-European tradition which was passed on through the influence of later International Gothic.

Masolino thus follows the more common and orthodox iconography of his own time and the two figures, in their gestures and postures, reflect a refined and courtly climate that contrasts with the episode by Masaccio opposite this fresco. Nevertheless, Masolino has endowed the figure of Adam with a "classical" quality which is of the purest beauty: his slightly pointed oval face framed by the locks of hair falling down over the nape of his neck and forehead, where they form a hollow around the temples, together with his strong nose and chin, all recall the features of Tiberius. The figure of Eve also has a sculptural quality in her body and a pearly light hovers over it, suggestive of a classical statue.

It was customary to distinguish the colouring of male bodies from female, the latter being fairer and more delicate. So Masolino uses a common base of a very light green mixed with yellow ochre, while the final colouring of Adam is stronger and darker, rather like that of Masaccio's Adam in the *Expulsion*.

The 18th-century insertion of a new arch at the entrance to the chapel led to the destruction of 33 centimetres at the top of the tree and the sky which probably appeared above the crown of the trees; at the same time an important area was also lost in the top right-hand corner, below the line of the impost of the capital. A copy was immediately painted in on new plaster, but this was removed during the restoration work; the scratch plaster below held signs of the original cartoon, so allowing the gap to be made good by restoring the forms with colouring that is closer to the original fresco. The black of the ground has suffered most of all, due to abrasions and the fact that it was laid on in an almost impalpable layer. It has also been whitened by widespread abrasion clearly caused by previous cleanings.

Masolino, Adam and Eve
in the Earthly Paradise
and The Temptation
*(during restoration). Pillar
to the right of the archway
leading into the chapel,
second order,* 214 × 89 cm.

Masaccio
The Expulsion from Eden

"Therefore the Lord God sent him forth from the garden of Eden, to till the ground from whence he was taken. So he drove out the man; and he placed at the east of the garden of Eden Cherubims, and a flaming sword which turned every way, to keep the way of the tree of life" (Genesis, 3, 23–24).

Man, though a sinner, has not lost his dignity in Masaccio's painting; he is not degraded or coarsened; the expressive beauty of his body is innovative in its expression yet recalls the archetypes of ideal classical beauty. The handling of the two figures contains suggestions of antiquity. In the case of Eve, there is a reminiscence of the Graeco-Roman *Venus pudica* which came down through Trecento models, though Masaccio's Eve retains only the gesture of a *Venus pudica*, with her heavy, deformed body and all the world's grief in her features and her dramatic gesture. The figure of Adam has been related to the *Laocoön* or the anatomical arrangement of the figures in the *Crucifixion* by Donatello in Santa Croce.

Golden rays emerge from the tall, narrow fissure of the foreshortened gate of the Garden, signifying the divine will that is expelling man after the act of sin; the command is reasserted by the angel whose left hand points to the path through the world.

In the outer world two dark, barren mounds seem to accompany the movement of the two figures: the one to the left, falling away sharply, follows the movement of Adam's left leg; the more rounded one on the right accompanies the ray of light, so reinforcing the dynamicity of the expulsion willed by the overwhelming divine power. Their shadows follow and mark out their laborious path towards the troubles of earthly life. The gravity of the episode banishes all superficiality. The intensity of the drama gives a tautness to the forms and culminates in the two heads: Adam's is bowed with his face sunk in his hands, as if in the conscious sorrow of reflection; Eve's head is thrown back and she cries out her anguish to the world.

This is one of the frescoes that has suffered most, due to the loss of the azure of the sky. After removing the dark monochrome wash laid on during restoration after the fire, all that was found was the greyish-blue of the ground laid on the fresh plaster. What might look like a defect or an error of execution of the greyish-blue colour of the sky surrounding the figure of Adam is actually merely evidence of the total loss of the original colour.

Masaccio, The Expulsion from Eden. *Pillar on the right of the entrance arch leading into the chapel, second order; 214 × 90 cm.*

Masaccio
The Tribute Money

"And when they were come to Capernaum, they that received tribute money came to Peter and said, Doth not your master pay tribute? He saith, Yes. And when he was come into the house, Jesus prevented him, saying, What thinkest thou, Simon? of whom do the kings of the earth take custom or tribute? of their own children, or of strangers? Peter saith to him, Of strangers. Jesus saith unto him, Then are the children free. Notwithstanding, lest we should offend them, go thou to the sea, and cast a hook, and take up the fish that first cometh up; and when thou hast opened his mouth, thou shalt find a piece of money: that take and give unto them for me and thee" (Matthew, 17, 24–27).

The *Tribute Money* is the most celebrated work in the whole chapel. Masaccio illustrates it in three stages in a single space: the demand for tribute and Jesus's immediate reply, as He shows Peter where to get the coin, occupies the centre; Peter catching the fish and finding the coin on the shore of the sea (actually Lake Gennesaret), on the left; Peter handing the coin to the tribute gatherer before his house, on the right.

The background to the central group is a mountain landscape which acquires different hues as it stretches away, ranging from the dark green of the planes in the foreground to the glimmers of snow in the distant planes of colour, ending in a whitish glow surmounted by a cloudy sky. The hills and mountains rising from the plain and studded with farmhouses, trees and hedges create a new sense of earthly space.

Of the apostles, the only ones that can be definitely identified are Peter (recognizable by the command Jesus is giving him and as he takes the coin from the fish and gives it to the tax gatherer) and John (recognizable by his closeness to Christ and his fair hair). The identification of the other ten is more difficult as none has his symbolic attributes, which of course entered iconography only after their martydom and the codification of their apostolates.

The figures are handled freely in the classical manner and are dressed in the "Greek" style: i.e. with the drapery

Masaccio, The Tribute Money.
Left wall, second order;
247 × 597 cm.

gathered in at the waist, hung over the left shoulder, enfolding the whole figure and slung over the left arm.

As for the state of preservation, the whole scene was one of those most severely damaged in the fire in 1771, so that the colouring is quite different from what it must have been originally. Nearly all the left-hand side of the scene tends towards reddish-brown in colour, destroying the effect of perspective which must originally have been created by the hues in *terre-verte*. The heat also seems to have modified some of the flesh tones, making them redder, as well as the yellow mantle of Saint Peter, laid on the ground by the lake. The fire was also the cause of the almost total loss of the original gilt decoration, which explains the absence of the early aureoles.

Masaccio
Saint Peter Preaching

"Ye men of Judaea, and all ye that dwell at Jerusalem, be this known unto you, and hearken to my words: Then Peter said unto them, Repent and be baptized every one of you in the name of Jesus Christ for the remission of sins, and ye shall receive the gift of the Holy Ghost. For the promise is unto you, and to your children, and to all that are afar off, even as many as the Lord our God shall call. And with many other words did he testify and exhort, saying, Save yourselves from this untoward generation. Then they that gladly received his word were baptized" (Acts, 2, 14, 38–41).

The episode lacks the profundity created by the oblique planes so often used by Masaccio. The crowd is packed together as in the fresco of *Saint Ivo Among the Wards* in Santo Stefano at Empoli: the mountains do not recede into infinity as in the *Tribute Money* or the *Baptism*, nor do they create space but rather weigh upon the figures. There is a definite link with the *Tribute Money*, but they are juxtaposed in an almost frontal position, without any scansion of pictorial space, with the trees almost disproportionate in relation to their placing. This episode has been transferred from the town to the countryside; it prepares for the *Baptism* which is painted on the same level on the same wall, to the right of the window.

There is an evident similarity of layout and distribution in the two works. Here too Peter is placed on the left, in profile, with his arm outstretched in a gesture emphasizing his words; here too there is a landscape which parallels the scene of the *Baptism of the Neophytes*. There are extensive alterations caused by the fire, which also caused the plaster to fall from the base of the painted pillar. In addition the fresco, painted as it was on the outer wall, though partly protected, was most affected by the heat as well as damaged by water seeping inside, and is hence extensively altered.

As with the *Baptism of the Neophytes*, the restoration revealed a scene hitherto completely unknown, with the recovery of remarkable features, like the wooded landscape which stretches away in profile against the horizon in a clear effort to create a spatial and temporal unity.

Masolino, Saint Peter Preaching.
*End wall on the left
of the window, second order;
247 × 168 cm.*

Masaccio
*The Baptism
of the Neophytes*

"Then they that gladly received His word were baptized: and the same day there were added unto them about three thousand souls" (Acts 11, 37–41).

The fresco shows twelve candidates for baptism plus Saint Peter, and as in the *Tribute Money* the apostles form a "Colosseum of men" so in this scene the figures create an endless procession that seems to stretch down the valley, beyond the painted pillar.

The cold flowing water of the stream covers the legs of the kneeling neophyte; the baptismal water is poured from the basin by Peter with the gesture of a sower onto the head of the young man, creating a myriad of bubbles and bathing his hair, then flowing into the water and leaving streams of bubbles also on the surface of the stream.

These are details that are difficult to perceive from below, as is the stubbly chin of one of the figures present at the baptism or the ear pressed by the turban.

Wholly new is the very fine figure in light blue who has been freed from repaintings and stands revealed as one of the "baptized" in the act of dressing again (he is just finishing buttoning up his clothing), while his hair is still wet.

The fresco has suffered most of all through the years and shows signs of the greatest loss of pigment. It has also been altered by the whitening caused by the decay of protein substances in it and the marked dulling of the colours by repaintings and the layers of fixatives applied in previous restorations.

*On the following page:
Masaccio,* The Baptism
of the Neophytes. *End wall
to the right of the window,
second order, 247 × 172 cm.*

Masolino
*The Healing
of the Lame Man
and The Raising
of Tabitha*

"Now Peter and John went up together to the temple at the hour of prayer, being the ninth hour. And a certain man lame from his mother's womb was carried, whom they laid daily at the gate of the temple which is called Beautiful, to ask alms of them that entered into the temple; Who seeing Peter and John about to go into the temple asked alms... Then Peter said, Silver and gold have I none; but such as I have give I thee: in the name of Jesus Christ of Nazareth rise up and walk. And he took him by the right hand... And he leaping up stood, and walked, and entering with them into the temple, walking, and leaping, and praising God" (Acts, 3, 1–10).

"Now there was at Joppa a certain disciple named Tabitha, which by way of interpretation is called Dorcas: this woman was full of good works and almsdeeds which she did. And it came to pass in those days, that she was sick, and died: whom when they had washed, they laid her in an upper chamber. And forasmuch as Lydda was nigh to Joppa, and the disciples had heard that Peter was there, they sent unto him two men, desiring him that he would not delay to come to them. Then Peter arose and went with them. When he was come, they brought him into the upper chamber: and all the widows stood by him weeping, and shewing the coats and garments which Dorcas made, while she was with them. But Peter put them all forth and kneeled down, and prayed; and turning him to the body said, Tabitha, arise. And she opened her eyes: and when she saw Peter she sat up. And he gave her his hand, and lifted her up, and when he had called the saints and widows, presented her alive" (Acts, 9, 36–41).

The two episodes are set by Masolino in a single place and in the same town, though historically they occurred at different times and places. On the left appears the episode of the healing of the lame man and on the right the resurrection of Tabitha.

Masolino, The Healing of the Lame Man and The Raising of Tabitha. *Right wall, second order; 247 × 588 cm.*

In the square at the centre of the scene, two elegantly-clothed figures divide yet link the two miracles, which are given the atmosphere of an everyday happening in the city

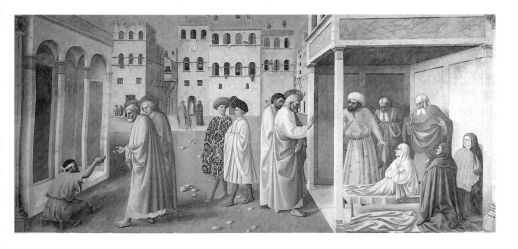

by the presence of these figures and those near the buildings. The scene looks just like a *piazza* in Florence.

For example, it might be a reprojection of Piazza della Signoria, if the temple porch on the right were taken as a reminiscence of the Loggia of Orcagna. Other features also enhance this sense of ordinariness: the vases on the window sills, the washing hung out to dry, the people at the windows, the brackets and horizontal poles on the buildings.

The fire did not greatly alter the colouring of this painting. Damage seems to be confined to the cornice at the bottom, the bench, the foot and a patch of ground below the lame man on the left, and the right side of the floor of the loggia. Variations and colour changes can, however, be found in the texture of the fresco and are related to the technique used and its deterioration caused by time.

Masaccio
*The Distribution
of the Goods
of the Community
and The Death
of Ananias*

"And the multitude of them that believed were of one heart and of one soul: neither said any of them that ought of the things which he possessed was his own; but they had all things common. And with great power gave the apostles witness of the resurrection of the Lord Jesus: and great grace was upon them all. Neither was there any among them that lacked; for as many as were possessors of lands or houses sold them, and brought the prices of the things that were sold, and laid them down at the apostles' feet; and distribution was made unto every man according as he had need. And Joses, who by the apostles was surnamed Barnabas (which is, being interpreted, The son of consolation), a Levite, and of the country of Cyprus, Having land, sold it, and brought the money and laid it at the apostles' feet.

"But a certain man named Ananias, with Saphira his wife, sold a possession, And kept back part of the price, his wife also being privy to it, and brought a certain part and laid it at the apostles' feet. But Peter said, Ananias, why has Satan filled thine heart to lie to the Holy Ghost, and to keep back part of the price of the land? Whilst it remained, was it not thine own? and after it was sold was it not in thine own power? why hast thou conceived this thing in thine heart? thou has not lied unto men, but unto God. And Ananias hearing these words fell down, and gave up the ghost: and great fear came on all them that heard these things. And the young men arose, wound him up, and carried him out, and buried him. And it was about the space of three hours after, when his wife, not knowing what was done, came in. And Peter answered unto her, Tell me whether ye sold the land for so much? And she said, Yea, for so much.

Then Peter said unto her, How is it that ye tempt the Spirit of the Lord? behold, the feet of them which have buried thy husband are at the door, and shall carry thee out. Then she fell down straightway at his feet, and yielded up the ghost" (Acts, 4, 32–37 and 5,1–10).

Masaccio gives the two key episodes of the story: the distribution of the goods by Saint Peter and the death of Ananias, whose body lies on the ground at his feet. The scene is set against the backdrop of the countryside beyond the houses. Apart from the stylistic reasons for varying the scene of *Saint Peter Healing with His Shadow*, this was probably due to the fact that the *Acts of the Apostles* mentions the sale of "land or houses."

The removal of dirt and the repainting of the fresco as part of its restoration did not create any differences in the parts that were renewed after the fire: but instead of effacing these sections that are not original it was decided to keep them, considering them a record of what was visible and existed before the fire rather than an arbitrary imaginary reconstruction.

Masaccio, The Distribution of the Goods
of the Community and The Death of Ananias.
*East wall to the right of the altar, first order,
232 × 157 cm.*

Masaccio
Saint Peter Healing with His Shadow

"And by the hands of the apostles were many signs and wonders wrought among the people... Insomuch that they brought forth the sick into the streets, and laid them on beds and couches, that at the least the shadow of Peter passing by might overshadow some of them. There came also a multitude out of the cities round about unto Jerusalem, bringing sick folks, and them which were vexed with unclean spirits: and they were healed every one" (Acts, 5, 12, 15–16).

In 1568 Vasari made a copy of the features of the man with the hood and used it as the portrait of Masolino at the beginning of the *Life* devoted to him. Since then critics have tried to identify other contemporary figures in this scene. Poggi (1903) noted the similarity between the bearded man with hands clasped and one of the Magi in the predella in Pisa but without suggesting an identity for him, a task taken up by others. Meller (1961) supposed it to be meant for Donatello; Berti (1966) thought Donatello was the bearded man between Saint Peter and Saint John; Parronchi thought the latter figure was Giovanni, the brother of Masaccio, known as "lo Scheggia," while Meller (1961) identified the youthful apostle with Masaccio himself.

The street-scene presented in perspective is lined not only by typical mediaeval Florentine houses but also a splendid stone-built palace: the lower part of this recalls the tall plinth of the Palazzo Vecchio on the side that slopes down to Via della Ninna, with its small recessed portico; while the upper part has windows framed with quoins which suggest the rhythms and proportions of Brunelleschi's Palazzo Pitti. The restoration that followed the fire covered up the alterations caused by the heat. These are now clearly evident in the whole of the left half of the stone-built palace, the lower part of the corner pilaster, the legs of the cripple and part of the ground. In these portions the original colours have been altered towards reddish tones, due to the oxidization of the yellow ochre and *terre-verte*. Part of the plasterwork that came away was re-applied to the wall in restoration after the fire while part of it was "badly repainted"; this was removed again from the wall and replaced in its true position, then linked to the rest of the composition by selective pictorial restoration.

On the following page:
Masaccio, Saint Peter Healing with His Shadow.
End wall to the left of the altar, first order, 232 × 162 cm.

Filippino Lippi
*Saint Peter Visited
in Prison by Saint Paul*

The *Golden Legend* tells that Theophilus, the prefect of Antioch, imprisoned Saint Peter. He would have certainly remained in prison had not Saint Paul, who visited him and cared for him, told Theophilus that Peter was capable of raising the dead. Theophilus replied that he would free Paul if he restored to life his son who died fourteen years earlier. Paul told Peter, who said: "This is a great miracle I am asked to perform, but the grace of God will do it for me. You have promised much, Paul, but everything is easy with the aid of God."

The fresco was attributed to Masaccio for many years. In reality it is the work by Lippi that most closely reflects Masaccio's style, to the point that it was supposed that Lippi was able to use the chalk lines previously drawn by Masaccio for an episode that the latter never completed as a fresco.

After the 1771 fire and the consequent restorations, it was noted, among other things, that "the colour of Saint Peter's tunic has greatly suffered, and the underlying leaden preparation has become visible... The red mantle is colourless... both Saint Peter and Saint Paul have golden aureoles, but they have been partially destroyed" (Cavalcaselle 1864).

Filippino Lippi, Saint Peter Visited in Prison by Saint Paul. *Left pilaster of the chapel entrance arch, first order, 232 × 89 cm.*

Masaccio
and Filippino Lippi
The Raising
of the Son of Theophilus
and Saint Peter
Enthroned

The *Golden Legend* (XLIV) narrates that Peter, was released from prison and brought before the open sepulchre of the young son of Theophilus, the prefect of Antioch, and with the aid of Saint Paul immediately raised the child, who had been dead for fourteen years.

Theophilus, all the people of Antioch and many others believed in God and built a magnificent church, and in the midst of it erected a throne where Peter could sit and be seen and heard by all.

Vasari tells us in the *Life* of Filippino Lippi that the artist worked on this fresco. "He (Lippi) in his youth completed the Brancacci Chapel in the church of the Carmine in Florence, begun by Masolino and not entirely finished by Masaccio on his death. So Filippo gave it its final form with his own hand and filled in the rest of a story that was incomplete, where Saint Peter and Saint Paul raise the nephew of the emperor (sic!); in the figure of this naked child he portrayed Francesco Granacci, then a young painter; and also portrayed Tommaso Soderini, *cavaliere*, Piero Guicciardini, father of *messer* Francesco that wrote the histories, Piero del Pugliese and Luigi Pulci, the poet."

In Masaccio's depiction the episode takes place out of doors in the presence of the people, before Theophilus seated on a throne.

In painting Saint Peter enthroned, Masaccio seems to have combined the two thrones, that of Antioch, to celebrate the miracle related in the *Legend*, and that of Rome, for the sake of the truth and universality that derive from it with the transfer of Peter and the foundation of the Church of which he was the first bishop.

The restoration of this fresco involved freeing the painted surface from substances overlaying it and preventing it from being seen properly; it also clearly confirmed the nature of the division of work between Masaccio and Filippino accepted by the critics.

The number of the personages seen on the right of Peter enthroned has been increased by one thanks to the recovery of a figure with a red cap, which had been covered up in repainting to make good the loss of some plaster, perhaps after the fire.

Masaccio and Filippino Lippi,
The Raising of the Son
of Theophilus and Saint Peter
Enthroned. *Left wall,*
first order, 232 × 597 cm.

Filippino Lippi
*Saint Peter Released
from Prison*

"Now about that time Herod the king stretched forth his hands to vex certain of the church. And he killed James the brother of John with the sword. And because he saw it pleased the Jews, he proceeded further to take Peter also. (Then were the days of the unleavened bread). And when he had apprehended him, he put him in prison, and delivered him to four quaternions of soldiers to keep him; intending after Easter to bring him forth to the people... And when Herod would have brought him forth, the same night Peter was sleeping between two soldiers, bound with two chains: and the keepers before the door kept the prison. And behold the angel of the Lord came upon him, and a light shined in the prison... And they went out, and passed on through one street and forthwith the angel departed from him" (Acts, 12, 1–10).

The scene shows Saint Peter awakened by the touch of the angels and led out of the prison, while the soldier is sleeping. It is significant that the artist has used dark, dull colours for the background and the soldier, while the apostle has a bright yellow mantle and the angel a white garment with a touch of light sky-blue, these being the colours that evoke the freedom lying before the two figures.

The state of the fresco is good on the whole, save for some partial losses made good in the 19th-century restoration, of which selections are here left (at the edge of the left-hand pillar; in the area around the hair and hands of the angel), the loss of colour in the top of the shaft of the soldier's spear and the feather in his hat, which was applied *a secco* on the previous day and so crumbled either because of the decomposition of the fixative or because of the cleanings it was subjected to after the fire in 1771.

Filippino Lippi, Saint Peter
Released from Prison.
*Pillar on the right arch
leading into the chapel,
first order, 232 × 89 cm.*

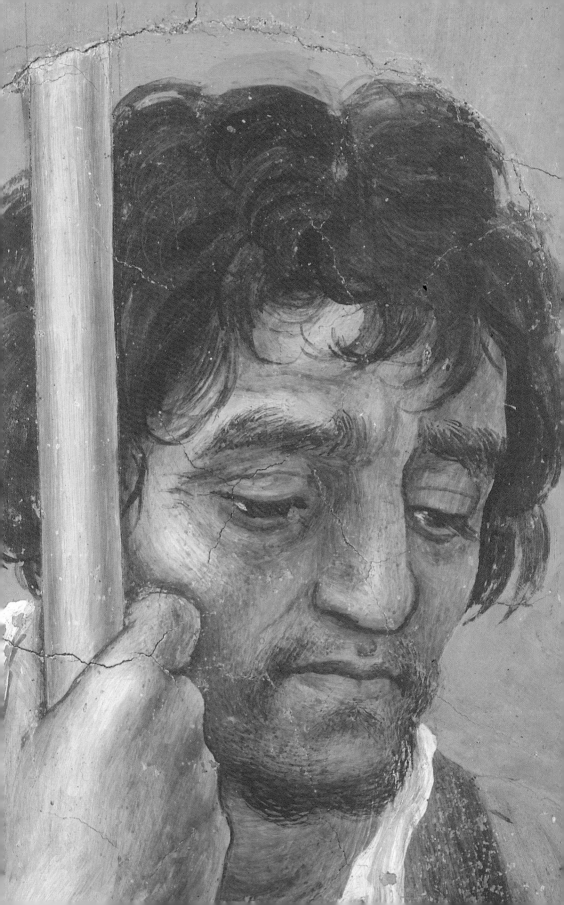

Filippino Lippi
The Dispute with Simon Magus and The Crucifixion of Saint Peter

The *Golden Legend* narrates that Simon Magus, a renowned magician in Jerusalem, where he had a great following, offered payment to Peter in exchange for the secrets of his powers; then he went to Rome, where, with his magic arts, he gained the trust of Nero. He challenged Peter and Paul to trials of skill, but was unable to raise the dead as they did.

Then Simon Magus, to revenge himself, threw himself from a tower and flew, sustained by devils. But Peter prayed that the devils might abandon him, and the magician plunged to the ground and was killed.

Later, at the height of the persecutions under Nero, Peter left Rome; but on the Appian Way Christ appeared to him. "Where are you going, Lord?," asked Peter. "I am going to Rome to be crucified a second time," was the reply. On hearing these words Peter understood that he was to return to the city and prepare for his martyrdom. And he was crucified upside-down, according to his own will, on the Janiculum.

On the right Peter and Paul are depicted disputing with Simon Magus before the Emperor, and on the left is the crucifixion of Saint Peter. Some theories hold that Masaccio had already painted the culminating scene of the martyrdom of Saint Peter and that it was destroyed to make way for the *Madonna of the People* on the altar. Then Filippino Lippi repainted the scene on this wall, which was still bare, when he was commissioned to complete the cycle and make good the damaged sections.

Here the painter has tried to place the episode within a precise historical context, going beyond the current iconography. The architecture of the walls and the gate, the impact of the walls with the pyramid, are presented as if copied from the real scene of Rome, as it still appears today despite the changes that have been made since then to the ancient Porta Ostiense, with the pyramid of Caius Cestius to the left (as seen from outside) and the Aurelian walls abutting onto it. Though the martyrdom of Peter did not take place here, the presence of the pyramid justifies the choice of setting.

Filippino Lippi, The Dispute with Simon Magus and The Crucifixion of Saint Peter. *Right wall, first order, 232 × 588 cm.*

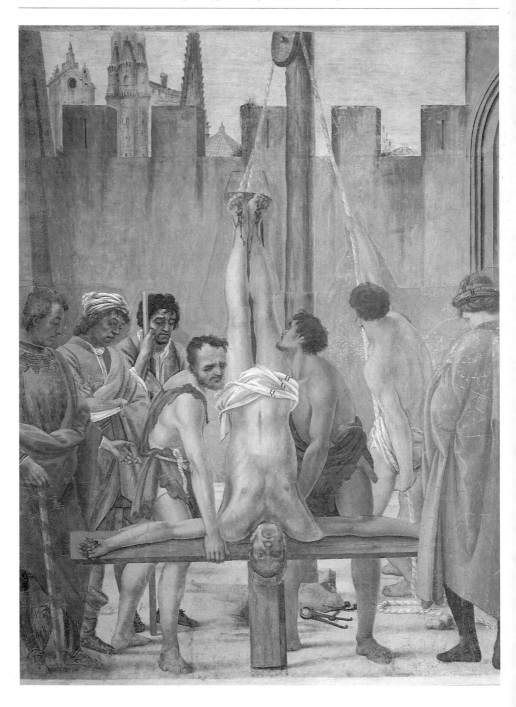

Vincenzo Meucci
The Madonna del Carmine

Vincenzo Meucci was already one of the most successful and prolific fresco painters in Tuscany when he received the commission to restore the Brancacci Chapel as part of the comprehensive project of embellishment to the church between 1746 and 1748. The cross vault was completely destroyed and replaced by a dome. Vincenzo Meucci decorated the new vault with the *Madonna Giving the Scapular to Saint Simon Stock*, while Carlo Sacconi decorated the lunettes with architectural motiifs.

The studies made before the restoration showed that it would be impossible to hope to recover any part of the structure of the ancient vault—and with it the frescoes of the Evangelists painted, according to the sources, by Masolino—because the new structure is set on a higher level than the old one.

During the renovation of the chapel after the fire (the work

was completed in 1782) the paintings by Meucci and Sacconi were restored by the will of Marchese Gabriele Riccardi, who had purchased the patronage of the chapel after the French descendents of the Brancacci family relinquished it. It was on this occasion that it was decided to record for posterity the miracle-working powers of the Madonna in the chapel that renewed the dedication of the church to the Madonna of Santa Maria del Carmine. On the shields of the two coats of arms in the spandrels of the vault by the entrance arch were inscribed the words *"signum salutis in periculis"* to commemorate the miraculous preservation from the flames in 1771 of the frescoes of Masaccio, Masolino, and Filippino Lippi.

The Restoration:
Research and Method

When the investigations and research were completed in November 1981, the following information had been collected: the whole of the original Gothic vault of the chapel had been destroyed by the reconstruction work in 1746–1748, which created a new cupola for Meucci's frescoes. It followed that there were no remnants of Masolino's frescoes in the vault and that also the round-headed arch above the original Gothic arch had been destroyed; the masonry base was quite sound and perfectly well preserved; following the removal of the whole of the lunettes, there was no trace below them of paintwork and very little trace of the Quattrocento *arriccio* or plaster base, so confirming that the frescoes were destroyed together with the plaster, and hence the *sinopie* or preparatory cartoons were also lost. That the cartoons did once exist is shown by the tiny fragments of plaster that still survive; following the removal of Meucci's frescoes below the *trompe l'œil* 18th century painted architecture, it was possible to recover two cartoons for the two stories lost in this section; the original mullioned window proved to have been reduced in size by raising the

level of the window sill, so enabling Masaccio to use the central section of this wall and the section above the mensa of the altar, where he painted a fresco whose position shows it was meant to serve as an altar painting. Fragments of this story, below a band of ornament that forms a cornice running under the window sill, reveal patches of landscape and a fragmentary figure to the right and other suggestions of figures to the left. They suggest that the scene represented was a story of Saint Peter, the final celebrated event in his life: the *Crucifixion*. This was the most important find, and quite unexpected, since there is no record of a scene of this kind placed at the top of the altar.

While these discoveries were coming to light, a series of analyses were also begun to supply the objective data that would indicate the most suitable methods to reclaim and restore the whole complex.

It is important to stress that the solutions to the historical, stylistic, documentary and analytic problems were followed by restoration work on the structure of the whole chapel, isolating it from external agents.

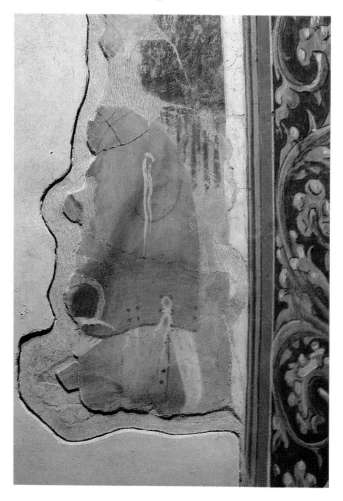

A complete summary of these analyses is listed here below: 1. photographic documentation through the use of direct lighting before the restoration of the frescoed sections; 2. photographic documentation using close lighting before the restoration of the frescoed sections; 3. examination of ultraviolet fluorescence. Executed before and after cleansing, this makes it possible to clearly identify the nature, extent and methods of intervention called for; 4. preliminary diagnostic examination using photographic infrared light. This makes it possible to gain further clues to the technique used by the artists, the nature of the pigments and possible rehandlings, additions, restoration work, etc.; 5. study of the micro-environment with particular reference to the proportion of sulphur dioxide in the air and the quantity and nature of the dust particles suspended in the air; in the latter case carbon particles were found to be abundant, and this explains the marked deterioration of the frescoes; 6. a study of the plasterwork, binding agents and the presence of mineral salts originating in the masonry and earlier interference with the frescoes. The methods used were chemical analysis and electron microscope scanning; 7. chemical-physical analysis, with the use of the new method for measuring sulphatization, the main cause of the deterioration of the frescoes; 8. studies using an instrument capable of analysing the wave-lengths of the light emanated by the frescoes so as to record the colours of the different sections before and after restoration and identify statistically the "disturbance" created by the dirt deposited on the surface; 9. infra-red spectrograph analysis. For the first time experimented and applied to the frescoed surfaces in the Brancacci Chapel, this method has enabled us to interpret the condition of the original pigment in the various levels of grey, and so predict the colour that would emerge after the dirt was removed; 10. micro-biological analysis of the walls conducted by sampling with swabs (moist or dry) and removing fragments with a scalpel. Direct aerobiological analysis to get some idea of the micro-biological content of the interior of the chapel and the wall surfaces; 11. double-exposure hologram investigation, capable of detecting deformities of the surfaces measuring fractions of a micron; 12. photogrammetrical studies for the construction of a graphico-numerical model of the frescoed walls so as to create an objective picture of their geometry and dimensions and identify features that are concealed or appear indistinct during direct examination; 13. thermographic studies, which provide information about the movement of heat between the walls and the interior, the construction of the chapel, variations in the materials used and the forces at work on it. This procedure showed up in an area where the plaster was detached from the masonry; further studies and analyses made it possible to preserve this area; 14. development of an appropriate cleaning technique which did not alter the pigments or the surface of the frescoes in any way while chemically removing the traces or organic substances, including the residues of earlier attempts at restoration.

This technique makes use of the ionic-exchanging proper-
ties of certain resins and the reactivity of ammonium car-
bonate; 15. designing a system to continually de-pollute the
interior "in real time" so as to prevent the arrival of harm-
ful agents in the chapel's atmosphere, especially when visi-
tors are present.

It is important to stress that the solutions to the historical,
stylistic, documentary and analytic problems were followed
by restoration work on the structure of the whole chapel,
isolating it from external agents. This was facilitated by the
ability to work freely in the adjacent rooms of the convent
which were also thoroughly restored and now form a secure
barrier against damage to the chapel and its interior.

Biographical Notes

Masolino Tommaso di Cristoforo Fini called
(Panicale in Valdelsa, 1383–Florence, 1440). Recorded by Vasari (1588) as a pupil of Ghiberti and his assistant on the first door of the Baptistry in Florence, he was enrolled in the Guild of Doctors and Apothecaries in 1423.
Although his training under Ghiberti cannot be considered certain, the late Gothic art of the goldsmith with its northern European accents, was primary influence on Masolino's development, along with the painting of Giovanni da Milano and that of Starnina, Lorenzo Monaco, and Gentile da Fabriano. Documents record the artist's presence in Florence in 1420 and 1422; the earliest work attributed to him is the *Madonna* now in the Kunsthalle in Bremen and dated 1423; on 2 November 1424 he was paid for the cycle of frescoes for the chapel of the Confraternity of Saint Helen in the Church of Santo Stefano degli Agostiniani at Empoli (Cole 1967–1968), a few fragments of which were found by Procacci (1953), including a *Pietà* (Museo della Collegiata) that reveals the influence of Masaccio. Also datable to 1424 is the *Madonna* now in the Alte Pinakotheke in Munich and the beginning of work on the panel for Sant'Ambrogio in Florence, depicting *Saint Ann with the Madonna and Child* (Uffizi) (Borsook 1981), which he painted in collaboration with Masaccio. On 8 July 1425 he was paid by the Confraternity of Saint Agnes for an unidentified work, and on 1 September left for Hungary, where he remained until 1427. Within this period (1425) is dated the *Carnesecchi Triptych* for Santa Maria Maggiore in Florence, now dismembered and partly lost; the *Scene from the Life of Saint Julian* (Montauban); the Saint Julian now in the Seminario Maggiore di Cestello in Florence, and the *Madonna and Child*, recorded by Toesca in Santa Maria at Novoli and stolen in 1923, appear to have belonged to this triptych. It is probable that prior to his departure for Hungary, and without subsequent interventions, he painted, together with Masaccio, the frescoes depicting *Scenes from the Life of Saint Peter* in the Chapel of Felice Brancacci in Santa Maria del Carmine. The time at which these were executed remains unclear, especially as far as Masolino is concerned, although recent studies and the restoration that is under way provide support for the hypothesis that both painters collaborated on the initial project. On 12 July 1427 Masolino is recorded as having received a commission for the Church of San Francesco at Figline Valdarno, but this may never have been carried out. However the artist is documented as being present in Florence on 18 May 1428, as well as in March 1429, though these may only represent short visits.
In Rome he frescoed the Branda Castiglione Chapel in the Basilica of San Clemente with *Scenes from the Life of Saint Catherine of Alexandria*, along with the large *Crucifixion* on the rear wall, whose composition and style sets it apart from the rest, and the *Annunciation* on the entrance wall. There is no further record of the painter until 1 November 1432, when he was paid for the fresco of the *Madonna and Child* in the Church of San Fortunato at Todi, which shows touches of Masaccio. The work is the last to be documented apart from the frescoes for the Collegiata in Castiglione Olona, which bear the date 1435. For this town, the birthplace of Cardinal Branda, Masolino painted the *Scenes from the Life of Saint John the Baptist* in the Baptistry and the *Scenes from the Life of the Virgin Mary* in the Collegiata, discovered in 1843, on which he was assisted by Paolo Schiavo (who remained there until 1436) and the Sienese painter Vecchietta, who may also have contributed to the cycle in the Baptistry. Having returned to Florence, the artist's death is recorded in the city's register on 18 October 1440. Still controversial are the attributions to him of the *Madonna and Child* now in Palazzo Vecchio; the small *Crucifixion* and *Death of the Virgin Mary* in the Pinacoteca Vaticana, perhaps part of the triptych in the Roman Church of Santa Maria Maggiore; and the *Madonna* now in Gloucester.

Masaccio, Tommaso di Giovanni Cassaio called
(San Giovanni Valdarno, 1401–Rome, 1428?). There is no stylis-

tic basis for the tradition mentioned by Vasari (1568) that he served his apprenticeship with Masolino. Nothing is known about the artist's education, but he was probably in Florence at an early age, where he is recorded as entering the Guild of Doctors and Apothecaries in 1422. Perhaps trained in a local workshop, as is suggested by the affinities with Mariotto di Cristofano, who married Masaccio's sister in 1422, the artist was equally influenced in his juvenile period by the current of "courtly" painting, represented in Florence in the 1420s by Gentile da Fabriano and Arcangelo di Cola da Camerino; however a decisive role must have been played by his encounter with the works of Giotto and Maso di Banco. The study of antiquity, common all the great painters of the Renaissance, was combined in Masaccio—as in Donatello and Brunelleschi—with an interest in perspective and natural features, creating the premises for his new style of painting. In the cloister of the Carmelite Church Masaccio painted the *Festival of the Consecration of the Church* (which took place on 19 April 1422), with portraits of various contemporaries in "green-earth": a number of late 16th-century drawings have been indicated as the only surviving testimonies of the work (Chiarini 1962). The panel painted for Sant'Ambrogio, depicting *Saint Ann with the Madonna and Child* (Uffizi), probably dates from 1424, after he had begun his artistic partnership with Masolino: Masaccio was undoubtedly responsible, as Longhi has pointed out (1940), for the *Child,* the *Madonna* and the *angel* at top right, while the rest of the painting is the work of Masolino. Subsequently the two artists worked together on the cycle of frescoes depicting *Scenes from the Life of Saint Peter* in the Felice Brancacci Chapel of the Carmelite Church, almost certainly painted at different times and finished by Masaccio alone. The last phase undoubtedly involved the design of the episodes that were later completed by Filippino Lippi. The unity of conception of the cycle, also revealed by the preparatory drawings that have been discovered (Baldini 1986), suggests a close collabora-

tion between the two masters, something that is also confirmed by recent studies. On 19 February 1426 Ser Giovanni di Colino degli Scarsi commissioned from Masaccio the polyptych for the Carmelite Church in Pisa, which was completed in December of the same year. All that remains of the work, described by Vasari and partly lost, is the central panel depicting the *Madonna Enthroned and Child* (London, National Gallery), the *Saint Paul* (Pisa, Museo Nazionale), the small *Crucifixion* in Naples (Galleria di Capodimonte), two scenes from the predella portraying the *Adoration of the Magi and the Martyrdom of Saint Peter and John the Baptist,* along with a few small panels of *Saints* now in Berlin (Staatliche Museen). As far as the sculptural character of his figures is concerned, the stay in Pisa had an important influence on Masaccio, both because of the presence of Donatello and Michelozzo in the city and because of the opportunity it gave him to study the work of Nicola Pisano and especially his son Giovanni, and the ancient marbles of the Camposanto. Masaccio probably painted the fresco of the *Trinity* in Santa Maria Novella in Florence for Domenico Lenzi, who died on 19 January 1426—as is recorded in the inscription. This was an unusual sepulchral monument serving as an altar. The extraordinary perspective layout of the vault has been attributed to Brunelleschi. The artist's presence in Florence on 29 July 1427 is documented, by the registration in the Cadastre. He later went to Rome, where together with Masolino he painted *Saints Jerome and John the Baptist* (London, National Gallery), part of the triptych of Santa Maria Maggiore, attributed to him by Clark (1951) and Longhi (1952), as well as by Vasari, who also ascribes to him the frescoes in the Branda Castiglione Chapel in San Clemente: in fact Longhi thinks that he can recognize the artist's hand in the horsemen of the scene depicting the *Crucifixion.*
Masaccio's death in Rome is recorded in the cadastral documents of 1429. Along with the above-mentioned works, it is worth citing the *Portrait of a Young Man* in Washington and the *Madonna and Child* in Palaz-

zo Vecchio, attributed to him by Longhi and probably painted after May 1426 (Del Bravo).
Still under discussion are the "desco da parte" in Berlin, the small *Scene from the Life of Saint Julian* in the Museo Horne, which has been linked by critics to Masolino's triptych for the Carnesecchi, and the *Madonna and Child* in Montemarciano, also attributed to Francesco d'Antonio.

Filippino Lippi
(Prato, 1457–Florence, 1504). The son of Filippo Lippi and Lucrezia Buti, he was in Spoleto with his father in the years 1467–1469. After Filippo's death he was entrusted to the care of Fra Diamante.
He is recorded in 1472 as Botticelli's assistant in Florence. Apart from a stay in Rome from 1488 to 1493 he spent the rest of his life in the Tuscan capital. His earliest output shows a close resemblance to Botticelli, to such an extent that some of these works were attributed to a painter known as "Amico di Sandro" (Sandro's friend). Between 1484 and 1485 he completed the frescoes in the Brancacci Chapel depicting *Scenes from the Life of Saint Peter,* adjusting his style to match that of Masaccio. A so-called late period commenced around 1484, when he painted the *Annunciation* in the San Gimignano Museum, which was followed by the *Madonna and Saints* (1486), the *Apparition of the Virgin to Saint Bernard* (1486), and the *Adoration of the Magi* (1496). During the Roman period he painted the frescoes in the Carafa Chapel in Santa Maria sopra Minerva, which became an emblem of the anti-classical tendencies that were emerging in Florence at the end of the Quattrocento. It was in fact the climate of crisis typical of Florence at the end of the century that inspired Filippino to produce works filled with an atmosphere of lyrical pietism (*Christ and the Virgin*). Although harshly judged in the past by critics, the last works that he painted (*Scenes from the Lives of Saint John the Evangelist and Saint Philip,* 1502, Strozzi Chapel in Santa Maria Novella) reveal an unusual theatrical and scenographic style and anticipate the themes and concepts of Mannerism.

Selected Bibliography

G. Vasari, *Le vite de' più eccellenti pittori, scultori ed architetti*, 3 vols., Florence 1568 (ed. edited by G. Milanesi, 9 vols., Florence 1878–1881; reprinted 1971).

A. Reumont, "Kappelle Brancacci. Masaccio und Filippino," in *Das Kunstblatt*, 1848, p. 117.

G. Rosini, *Sulle pitture di Masaccio nella Cappella Brancacci, etc.*, Pisa 1848.

J.A. Crowe, G.B. Cavalcaselle, *A New History of Painting in Italy from the Second to the Sixteenth Century*, London 1864–1871.

A.H. Layard, *The Brancacci Chapel*, London 1868.

G. Milanesi, "Sulle pitture della Cappella Brancacci," in *Le Vite di G. Vasari*, tomo II, Florence 1878, pp. 305 ff.

B. Marrai, " Gli affreschi della Cappella Brancacci al Carmine," in *Arte e Storia*, 1891, 10 April, pp. 59–60.

A. Bayersdorfer, " Masaccio und Filippino, Fresken in der Brancacci Kapelle," in *Leben und Schriften aus seinem Nachlass*, 1902, pp. 56–58.

M.K. Kreutz, *Masaccio*, Berlin 1902.

G. Poggi, "La tavola di Masaccio per il Carmine di Pisa," in *Miscellanea d'Arte*, October–November 1903, pp. 145–191.

G.P. Konody, *Filippino Lippi*, London 1905.

G. Sortais, "Masaccio et la Chapelle Brancacci," in *Etudes*, 1905, XLII, tomo 104, pp. 343–371.

P. Toesca, *Masolino da Panicale*, Bergamo 1908.

J. Mesnil, "Per la storia della Cappella Brancacci," in *Rivista d'Arte*, 1912, VII, p. 34; VIII, pp. 34–40.

O.H. Giglioli, *Masaccio*, Florence 1921.

E. Somaré, *Masaccio*, Milan 1924.

A. Schmarsow, *Masolino und Masaccio*, Leipzig 1928.

O.H. Giglioli, " Masaccio" (comparative bibliographical essay), in *Bollettino del Real Istituto di Architettura e Storia dell'Arte*, 1929, III, pp. 55–101.

U. Mengin, *Les deux Lippi*, Paris 1929.

M. Salmi, " L'autoritratto di Masaccio nella Cappella Brancacci," in *Rivista Storica Carmelitana*, 1929, pp. 99 ff.

H. Brockhaus, "Die Brancacci-Kapelle in Florenz," in *Mitteilungen des Kunsthistoriches Institutes in Florenz*, 1930, III, pp. 160–182.

U. Procacci, "L'incendio della chiesa del Carmine del 1771. La Sagra di Masaccio. Gli affreschi della cappella di San Giovanni," in *Rivista d'Arte*, 1932, XIV, pp. 141–232.

U. Procacci, "Relazione dei lavori eseguiti nella chiesa del Carmine di Firenze per la ricerca di antichi affreschi," in *Bollettino d'Arte del Ministero della Pubblica Istruzione*, 1933–1934, XXVII, pp. 327–334.

M. Pittaluga, *Masaccio*, Florence 1935.

K.B. Neilson, *Filippino Lippi*, Cambridge (Mass.) 1938.

R. Longhi, "Fatti di Masolino e di Masaccio," in *Critica d'Arte*, 1940, 3–4, pp. 145–191.

U. Procacci, "La Cappella Brancacci. Vicende storiche," in *La Cappella Brancacci. Quaderni di restauro*, 1944, I, pp. 9 ff.

M. Salmi, *Masaccio*, Milan (2nd ed.) 1948.

K. Steinbart, *Masaccio*, Vienna 1948.

A. Scharf, *Filippino Lippi*, Vienna 1950.

K. Clark, "An Early Quattrocento Triptych from Santa Maria Maggiore, Roma," in *Burlington Magazine*, 1951, pp. 339–347.

U. Procacci, *Masaccio*, Milan 1951 (2nd ed. 1952).

R. Longhi, "Presenza di Masaccio nel trittico della Neve," in *Paragone*, 1952, 25, pp. 8–16.

U. Procacci, "Sulla cronologia delle opere di Masaccio e di Masolino tra il 1425 e il 1428," in *Rivista d'Arte*, 1953, pp. 3–55.

U. Procacci, "Il Vasari e la conservazione degli affreschi della Cappella Brancacci al Carmine e della Trinità in S. Maria Novella," in *Scritti in onore di L. Venturi*, Rome 1956, pp. 211–222.

L. Berti, U. Baldini, *Filippino Lippi*, Florence 1957.

F. Gamba, *Filippino Lippi nella storia della critica*, Florence 1958 (with extensive bibliography).

E. Micheletti, *Masolino da Panicale*, Milan 1959.

P. Meller, "La Cappella Brancacci. Problemi ritrattistici e iconografici," in *Acropoli*, 1961, III, pp. 186 ff.; IV, pp. 273 ff.

E. Chiarini, "Una citazione della 'Sagra' di Masaccio nel Ghirlandaio," in *Paragone*, 1962 149, pp. 53–55 and figs. 54–56.

L. Berti, *Masaccio*, Milan 1964.

F. Bologna, *Gli affreschi della Cappella Brancacci*, Milan 1965.

C. De Tolnay, "Note sur l'iconographie des fresques de la Chapelle Brancacci," in *Studi in onore di Giusta Nicco Fasola*, in *Arte Lombarda*, 1965, X, pp. 69 ff.

U. Procacci, *Masaccio e la Cappella Brancacci*, Florence 1965.

L. Berti, "Donatello e Masaccio," in *Antichità Viva*, 1966, V, 3, pp. 3–12.

A. Parronchi, *Masaccio*, Florence 1966.

L. Berti, *L'opera completa di Masaccio*, Milan 1968.

M. Chiarini, *Masaccio e la pittura del Quattrocento in Toscana*, Milan 1968.

C. Del Bravo, Masaccio, *Tutte le opere*, Florence 1969.

L.B. Watkins, "Technical Observation on the Frescoes of the Brancacci Chapel," in *Mitteilungen des Kunsthistorisches Institutes in Florenz*, 1973, pp. 68–74.

R. Longhi, "Fatti di Masolino e di Masaccio e altri studi sul Quattrocento," in *Opere complete di Roberto Longhi*, VIII/1 Florence 1975, pp. 3–65.

U. Procacci, "Nuove testimonianze su Masaccio," in *Commentari*, 1976, 27, pp. 223–237.

A. Molho, "The Brancacci Chapel: Studies in its Iconography and History," in *Journal of the Warburg and Courtauld Institutes*, 1977, XL, pp. 50–98.

B. Amaducci, *La Cappella Brancacci e l'opera di Masaccio*, Florence 1978.

A.M. Petrioli Tofani, *Masaccio*, Florence 1978.

Eiko M.L. Wakayama, "Lettura iconografica degli affreschi della Cappella Brancacci: analisi dei gesti e della composizione," in *Commentari*, 1978, 1–4, pp. 72–80.

E. Borsook, *The Mural Painters of Tuscany*, Oxford, 2nd ed., 1989.

B. Cole, *Masaccio and the Art of*

Early Renaissance Florence, Bloomington and London 1980.

U. Procacci, *Masaccio*, Florence 1980.

L.B. Watkins, *The Brancacci Chapel Frescoes: Meaning and Use* (1976), Ann Arbor 1981.

U. Baldini, "Nuovi affreschi nella Cappella Brancacci. Masaccio e Masolino," in *Critica d'Arte*, 1984, XLIX, 1, pp. 65–72.

U. Procacci, U. Baldini, "La Cappella Brancacci nella chiesa del Carmine a Firenze," in *Quaderni del restauro*, 1984, 1, pp. 9– 2, 20.

O. Casazza, "Il ciclo delle Storie di San Pietro e la 'Historia Salutis'. Nuova lettura della Cappella Brancacci," in *Critica d'Arte*, 1986, LI, 9, pp. 69–84.

O. Casazza, "Settecento nella Cappella Brancacci," in *Critica d'Arte*, 1986, 11, pp. 66, 68–72.

U. Baldini, "Restauro della Cappella Brancacci, primi risultati," in *Critica d'Arte*, 1986, IX, pp. 65–68.

E. Colle, *Masaccio*, Montepulciano 1987.

L. Pandimiglio, "Felice di Michele vier clarissimus e una consorteria: i Brancacci di Firenze," in *Quaderni di restauro*, 1987, 3.

U. Baldini, in *I pittori della Brancacci agli Uffizi*, Florence 1988.

U. Baldini, "Le figure di Adamo e Eva formate affatto ignude in una cappella di una principale chiesa di Fiorenza," in *Critica d'Arte*, 1988, LIII, no. 16, pp. 72–77.

L. Berti, *Masaccio*, Florence 1988.

C. Caneva, "L'ultimo della Brancacci," in *Gli Uffizi. Studi e Ricerche*, 1988, no. 5, pp. 85 ff.

U. Baldini, "Dalla scoperta di San Giovenale a quella della Brancacci," in *Gli Uffizi. Studi e Ricerche*, 1989, no. 5, pp. 16–18.

U. Baldini, Del "'Tributo' e altro di Masaccio," in *Critica d'Arte*, 1989, LIV, no. 20, pp. 29–38.

L. Berti, R. Foggi, *Masaccio*, Florence 1989.

O. Casazza, "La documentazione grafica della Cappella Brancacci," in O. Casazza, P. Cassinelli Lazzeri, *La Cappella Brancacci, conservazione e restauro nei documenti della grafica antica*, Modena 1989.

O. Casazza, P. Cassinelli Lazzeri, *La Cappella Brancacci, conservazione e restauro nei documenti della grafica antica*, Modena 1989.

P.A. Rossi, "Lettura del Tributo di Masaccio," in *Critica d'Arte*, 1989, LIV, n. 20, pp. 39–42.

O. Casazza, *Masaccio e la Cappella Brancacci*, Florence 1990.

U. Baldini, O. Casazza, *La Cappella Brancacci*, Milan 1990.

This guide was printed by Elemond S.p.a.
at the plant in Martellago (Venice)